FAVORITE CROCHETED TABLECLOTH DESIGNS

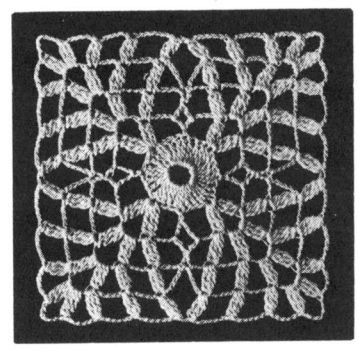

Edited by Rita Weiss

Dover Publications, Inc., New York

CROCHET ABBREVIATIONS

ch . . . . chain
sc . . . . . . single crochet
half dc . . . . half double crochet
dc . . . . . double crochet
tr . . . . treble
d tr . . . . . double treble
sl st . . . . slip stitch

pc st . . . popcorn stitch
sp . . . . space
st(s) . . . . stitch(es)
rnd . . . . round
incl . . . . inclusive
inc . . . . increase
dec . . . . decrease

* (asterisk) or † (dagger) . . . Repeat the instructions following the asterisk or dagger as many times as specified.

** or †† . . . Used for a second set of repeats within one set of instructions.

Repeat instructions in parentheses as many times as specified. For example: **"(Ch 5, sc in next sc) 5 times"** means to work all that is in parentheses 5 times.

Copyright © 1985 by Dover Publications, Inc.
All rights reserved under Pan American and International Copyright Conventions.

Published in Canada by General Publishing Company, Ltd., 30 Lesmill Road, Don Mills, Toronto, Ontario.

Published in the United Kingdom by Constable and Company, Ltd., 10 Orange Street, London WC2H 7EG.

This Dover edition, first published in 1985, is a new selection of patterns from *Tablecloths, Heirlooms of Tomorrow, Book No. 251*, published by The Spool Cotton Company in 1949; *The Newest in Tablecloths and Bedspreads, Book No. 295*, published by The Spool Cotton Company in 1952; *Decorative Crochet to Enhance Your Home, Book 46*, published by Royal Society, Inc., in 1938; *Heirlooms to Crochet, Book No. 48*, published by Royal Society, Inc., in 1939; *Hand Crochet by Royal Society, Book No. 4*, published by Royal Society, Inc., in 1945; *Treasure Chest of Crochet, Star Book No. 45*, published by American Thread Company in 1946. A new introduction has been especially written for this edition.

Manufactured in the United States of America
Dover Publications, Inc., 31 East 2nd Street, Mineola, N.Y. 11501

Library of Congress Cataloging in Publication Data

Main entry under title:

Favorite crocheted tablecloth designs.

   1. Crocheting—Patterns. 2. Tablecloths. I. Weiss, Rita.
TT825.F38 1985   746.9'6   84-21090
ISBN 0-486-24873-9 (pbk.)

INTRODUCTION

Most of those elegant crocheted tablecloths found in antique shops today were created from designs produced by America's thread companies during the early part of this century. These designs were disseminated to the public through the ten-cent leaflets the companies published as a marketing device for selling their crochet threads. Literally thousands of leaflets, offering instructions for all kinds of crocheted and knitted items, were produced over a fifty-year period.

An entire industry evolved to create designs, write directions, make models, and produce leaflets. (The crocheting of models was usually done by a bevy of women working in their homes.) Design directors such as Anne Orr, Cecilia Vanek, and others had entire staffs whose sole job was to produce more and more beautiful patterns using the manufacturers' threads.

Then, the vogue for crocheted lace disappeared; it became cheaper—and certainly quicker—to purchase machine-made lace tablecloths. In turn, the thread companies began to concentrate on products other than crochet thread. As huge conglomerates devoured the smaller companies, new management took over and instigated marketing techniques which did not include spending money on design departments and the publication of leaflets. Company offices were consolidated, rents rose, and as space sold at a premium the "old crocheted rags in the back room" had to be moved, doubtless to make way for the new computer. In a fit of housecleaning, many of the original models were destroyed, probably by a modern marketing director who did not realize he was destroying masterpieces.

With the current popularity of handmade items, there is once again a need for patterns. Today's economics, however, do not permit thread companies to produce leaflets merely to sell thread; the leaflets must themselves be profitable. The 10¢ leaflet is now a $3.00 book, and the original old leaflets with their magnificent designs have become sought-after collector's items.

This book contains some of the best tablecloth designs as they were originally shown in the old instructional leaflets. Many of the threads listed in the patterns are still available. We must, however, caution you that some product names used on threads a quarter-century ago are today being reused on different materials. When in doubt, check with the local knitting shop. Most important: **Whatever type of thread used, be sure to obtain the same gauge as in the original pattern**. Also, purchase sufficient amount of the same dye lot to complete the project. It is often impossible to match shades later as dye lots vary.

For perfect results, the number of stitches and rows should correspond to those indicated in the directions. Before starting your tablecloth, make a small sample of the stitch working with the suggested hook size and desired thread. If your working tension is too tight or too loose, change to a larger or smaller crochet hook, as necessary, to obtain the correct gauge.

When you have completed your tablecloth, wash and block it. Use warm water and a good neutral soap or detergent. Squeeze the suds through the tablecloth, then rinse in clear water. Following the measurements given with the directions, with rust-proof pins, pin the tablecloth right side down on a well-padded surface. Pin out all picots, loops, and scallops. When the tablecloth is completely dry, steam press with a damp cloth, but do not allow the iron to rest on the stitches. Let the steam do the work.

The crochet terminology and hooks listed in this book are those used in the United States. The following charts give the U.S. names of the crochet stitches and their equivalents in other countries, plus the equivalents to U.S. crochet hook sizes. Crocheters should become thoroughly familiar with the difference in both terms and hook sizes before beginning any project.

All of the stitches used in this book are explained on page 47.

STITCH CONVERSION CHART

U.S. Name	Equivalent
Chain	Chain
Slip	Single crochet
Single crochet	Double crochet
Half-double or short-double crochet	Half-treble crochet
Double crochet	Treble crochet
Treble crochet	Double-treble crochet
Double-treble crochet	Treble-treble crochet
Treble-treble or long-treble crochet	Quadruple-treble crochet
Afghan stitch	Tricot crochet

HOOK CONVERSION CHART

Aluminum

U.S. Size	B	C	D	E	F	G	H	I	J	K
British & Canadian Size	12	11	10	9	8	7	5	4	3	2
Metric Size	2½	3	—	3½	4	4½	5	5½	6	7

Steel

U.S. Size	00	0	1	2	3	4	5	6
British & Canadian Size	000	00	0	1	—	1½	2	2½

Leafy Bower

60 x 80 Inches

MATERIALS: J. & P. Coats or Clark's O.N.T. Best Six Cord Mercerized Crochet, Size 50, *White only:*
Small Ball: J. & P. Coats—*82 balls,* or Clark's O.N.T. —*122 balls* . . . Steel Crochet Hook No. 12.

GAUGE: Each motif measures 2⅜ inches square.

FIRST MOTIF . . . Starting at center, ch 12. Join with sl st to form ring. **1st rnd:** Ch 4, 31 tr in ring. Sl st in top of ch-4. **2nd rnd:** Ch 4, holding back on hook the last loop of each tr make 2 tr in same place as sl st, thread over and draw through all loops on hook (cluster made), * ch 5, make a 3-tr cluster in same st as last cluster was made, ch 7, skip 3 tr, sc in next tr, ch 7, skip 3 tr, 3-tr cluster in next tr. Repeat from * around, ending with ch 7, sl st in first cluster. **3rd rnd:** Ch 4, 2-tr cluster in same place as sl st, * ch 4, in next sp make 3-tr cluster, ch 5 and 3-tr cluster; ch 4, cluster in tip of next cluster, ch 5, holding back on hook the last loop of each dc make dc in next 2 sps, thread over and draw through all loops on hook (joint dc made), ch 5, cluster in tip of next cluster. Repeat from * around. Join. **4th rnd:** Ch 4, 2-tr cluster in same place as sl st, * ch 5, cluster in tip of next cluster, ch 5, in next sp make cluster, ch 5 and cluster; (ch 5, cluster in tip of next cluster) twice, ch 5, (sc in next sp) twice; ch 5, cluster in tip of next cluster. Repeat from * around. Join. **5th rnd:** Ch 4, 2-tr cluster in same place as sl st, * (ch 6, cluster in tip of next cluster) twice; ch 5, in next sp make cluster, ch 6 and cluster; ch 5, (cluster in tip of next cluster, ch 6) twice; (cluster in tip of next cluster) twice. Repeat from * around. Join and break off.

SECOND MOTIF . . . Work as for First Motif until 4th rnd is completed. **5th rnd:** Ch 4, 2-tr cluster in same cluster, (ch 6, cluster in tip of next cluster) twice; ch 5, cluster in next sp, ch 3, sl st in corresponding sp on First Motif, ch 3, cluster in same sp on Second Motif as last cluster was made, ch 2, sl st in corresponding sp on First Motif, ch 2, (cluster in tip of next cluster on Second Motif, ch 3, sl st in corresponding sp on First Motif, ch 3) twice; (cluster in tip of next cluster on Second Motif) twice; (ch 3, sl st in corresponding sp on First Motif, ch 3, cluster in tip of next cluster on Second Motif) twice; ch 2, sl st in corresponding sp on First Motif, ch 2, cluster in next sp on Second Motif, ch 3, sl st in corresponding sp on First Motif, ch 3, cluster in same sp on Second Motif as last cluster was made and complete rnd as for First Motif.

Make 25 rows of 32 motifs, joining adjacent sides as Second Motif was joined to First Motif (where 4 corners meet, join 3rd and 4th corners to joining of previous 2 corners).

EDGING . . . Attach thread in tip of any cluster, sc in same place, ch 4, sl st in sc (picot made); * 5 sc in next sp, in tip of next cluster make sc, ch 4, sl st in sc (for picot). Repeat from * around. Join and break off.

The beauty of handmade lace is timeless—here its enduring charm finds new expression.

Remembrance

MATERIALS:
    Royal Society Six Cord Cordichet, *Small Ball*, size 20, 8 boxes of *White or Beige*, or 9 boxes of *Ecru*; or
    Royal Society Six Cord Cordichet, *Large Ball*, size 20, 3 boxes of *White or Beige*.

Milward's steel crochet hook No. 9 or 10.

Each motif measures 5½ inches in diameter.

Motif . . . ch 5, join with sl st. **1st rnd:** ch 4 (to count as 1st tr of cluster); make 2 tr in ring, holding back the last loop of each tr on hook; * thread over and draw through all loops, ch 1 tightly (cluster completed); ch 3 more, 3 tr in ring, holding back the last loop of each tr on hook. Repeat from * until 8 clusters are made. Ch 3, join to tip of 1st cluster. **2nd rnd:** sl st in next 2 ch, sc in sp, * ch 6, sc in next sp, ch 3, sl st in top of sc just made (p). Repeat from *; end with p, join. **3rd rnd:** sl st to 3rd ch of 1st loop, sc in loop, * ch 11, sc in next loop. Repeat from *, joining to starting sc. **4th rnd:** sl st in next 3 ch, * 7 sc in loop, ch 5. Repeat from *; join. **5th rnd:** ch 3, dc in next 6 sc, 6 dc under ch-5, * dc in 7 sc, 6 dc under ch-5 (104 dc). Repeat from *; join. **6th rnd:** ch 3, dc in each dc around, making 2 sts in 1 st directly above each of 4 ch-11 loops of 3rd rnd (108 dc); join. **7th rnd:** * ch 7, sk 3 dc, sc in next dc, ch 7, sk 4 dc, sc in next dc. Repeat from * around; join (24 loops). **8th rnd:** sl st to 3rd ch, sc in loop, * ch 7, in center ch of next ch-7 make sc, ch 3 and sc. Repeat from * around, ending with sc, ch 3; join. **9th rnd:** sl st to center of loop, sc in loop, * ch 7, sc in next loop. Repeat from *; join. **10th rnd:** * in ch-7 make sc, h dc, dc, 5 tr, dc, h dc, sc; sl st in sc. Repeat from *; join. **11th rnd:** sl st to center tr, sc in center tr, * ch 4; in center tr of next scallop make tr, ch 2, tr, ch 5, tr, ch 2, tr; ch 4, sc in center st of next scallop. Repeat from *; join. Fasten off.

Make another motif like this to within last rnd. **Last rnd:** sl st to center tr, * sc in center tr, ch 4, in center tr of next scallop make tr, ch 2, tr, ch 2; drop loop from hook, insert hook in center ch of a ch-5 at tip of any scallop of 1st motif; draw loop through; ch 2, make tr, ch 2 and tr back in same st on motif in work, ch 4. Repeat from * once; complete rnd without any additional joinings.

For a tablecloth 72 × 90 inches, 13 motifs across and 16 down.

Fill-in-lace . . . Ch 5, join with sl st. **1st rnd:** ch 4 (to count as 1st tr of cluster); 2 tr in ring, holding back the last loop of each tr on hook; thread over and draw through all loops, ch 1 tightly. Ch 7, drop loop from hook, insert hook in ch-5 sp at tip of a free scallop between joinings and draw loop through; ch 7, 3-tr cluster in ring, ch 19, insert hook at joining of next 2 scallops, and complete joining as before; ch 19, 3-tr cluster in ring, ch 7, join to next free scallop, ch 7, 3-tr cluster in ring, ch 19. Continue thus, joining last ch-19 at base of 1st ch-7. Fasten off securely. Fill in all spaces in this manner.

Bridesmaid's Bouquet

60 x 80 Inches

MATERIALS: J. & P. Coats Big Ball Best Six Cord Mercerized Crochet, Size 30: 42 balls of White, Ecru or Cream, or 52 balls of any color, or Clark's Big Ball Three Cord Mercerized Crochet, Size 30: 30 balls of White, Ecru or Cream, or 42 balls of any color ... Steel Crochet Hook No. 10.

GAUGE: Each motif measures 2½ inches in diameter.

FIRST MOTIF ... Starting at center, ch 7. Join with sl st to form ring. **1st rnd:** 18 sc in ring. Sl st in first sc. **2nd rnd:** Ch 4, dc in next sc, (ch 1, dc in next sc) 16 times; ch 1, sl st in 3rd ch of ch-4. **3rd rnd:** Ch 3, * dc in next sp, dc in next dc. Repeat from * around. Join. **4th rnd:** Ch 4, * dc in next dc, ch 1. Repeat from * around. Join. **5th rnd:** Ch 3, * skip next dc, in next dc make dc, ch 5 and dc. Repeat from * around, ending with dc in sl st of previous rnd, ch 2, dc in top of ch-3 (18 loops). **6th rnd:** Ch 3, * dc in next loop, ch 6, dc in same loop. Repeat from * around, ending with ch 6, sl st in top of ch-3. **7th rnd:** * In next loop make 2 sc, dc, ch 5, dc and 2 sc; in next loop make 2 sc, dc, ch 3, dc and 2 sc. Repeat from * around. Sl st in first sc. Break off.

SECOND MOTIF ... Work as for First Motif until 6th rnd is completed. **7th rnd:** 2 sc in next loop, dc in same loop, ch 2, sl st in corresponding ch-5 loop on First Motif, ch 2, make dc and 2 sc in same loop on Second Motif as last dc was made, make 2 sc and dc in next loop, ch 1, sl st in next ch-3 loop on First Motif, ch 1, make dc and 2 sc in same loop on Second Motif as last dc was made, make 2 sc and dc in next loop, ch 2, sl st in next ch-5 loop on First Motif, ch 2, make dc and 2 sc in same loop on Second Motif as last dc was made and complete rnd as for First Motif (no more joinings).

Make 14 rows of 34 motifs and 13 rows of 33 motifs, joining corresponding loops of adjacent sides as Second Motif was joined to First Motif. See page 15.

Sweet Clover

60 x 75 Inches

MATERIALS: J. & P. Coats Big Ball Best Six Cord Mercerized Crochet, Size 30: 46 balls of White, Ecru or Cream, or 57 balls of any color, or Clark's Big Ball Three Cord Mercerized Crochet, Size 30: 33 balls of White, Ecru or Cream, or 46 balls of any color ... Steel Crochet Hook No. 10.

GAUGE: Each motif measures 2½ inches square.

FIRST MOTIF . . . Starting at center, ch 8. Join with sl st to form ring. **1st rnd:** Ch 3, 23 dc in ring. Sl st in top of ch-3. **2nd rnd:** Ch 10, * skip 1 dc, tr in next dc, (ch 3, skip 1 dc, tr in next dc) twice; ch 6. Repeat from * around, ending with ch 3, sl st in 4th st of ch-10. **3rd rnd:** Sl st to sp, ch 4, 4 tr in same sp, * ch 5, 5 tr in same sp, ch 3, skip next sp, dc in next tr, ch 3, skip next sp, 5 tr in next sp. Repeat from * around. Sl st in top of ch-4. **4th rnd:** Ch 4, tr in next 4 tr, * ch 4, in corner sp make 5 tr, ch 3 and 5 tr; ch 4, tr in next 5 tr, ch 3, skip 2 sps, tr in next 5 tr. Repeat from * around. Join as before. **5th rnd:** Ch 4, holding back on hook the last loop of each tr make tr in next 4 tr, thread over and draw through all loops on hook (cluster made), * ch 8, sc in next sp, ch 6, cluster over next 5 tr as before, ch 7, 5-tr cluster in corner sp, ch 7, cluster over next 5 tr, ch 6, sc in next sp, ch 8, (cluster over next 5 tr) twice. Repeat from * around. Sl st in first cluster. Break off.

SECOND MOTIF . . . Work as for First Motif until 4th rnd is completed. **5th rnd:** Ch 4, and complete cluster as before, * ch 8, sc in next sp, ch 6, cluster over next 5 tr, ch 7, 5-tr cluster in corner sp, ch 3, sl st in corresponding loop on First Motif, ch 3, cluster over next 5 tr on Second Motif, ch 3, sl st in corresponding loop on First Motif, ch 3, sc in next sp on Second Motif, ch 4, sl st in corresponding loop on First Motif, ch 4, (cluster over next 5 tr on Second Motif) twice; ch 4, sl st in corresponding loop of First Motif, ch 4, sc in next sp on Second Motif, ch 3, sl st in corresponding loop of First Motif, ch 3, cluster over next 5 tr on Second Motif, ch 3, sl st in corresponding loop of First Motif, ch 3, 5-tr cluster in corner sp on Second Motif and complete rnd as for First Motif.

Make 24 rows of 30 motifs, joining adjacent sides as Second Motif was joined to First Motif.

EDGING . . . Attach thread in corner cluster of corner motif, ch 5, sl st in 5th ch from hook (picot made), * ch 4, sc in next loop, ch 4, sc in tip of next cluster, ch 4, sl st in last sc made (another picot made), (ch 4, sc in next loop) twice; ch 4, sc between next 2 clusters, picot, (ch 4, sc in next loop) twice; ch 4, sc in tip of next cluster, picot, ch 4, sc in next sp, ch 4, sc in tip of next cluster, picot, ch 6, sc in tip of first free cluster on next motif, picot. Repeat from * around. Join and break off.

Picture a gossamer web on your dark, polished table top and you will vision the effect of this lacy filigree-like cloth.

Filigree

MATERIALS:

ROYAL SOCIETY SIX CORD CORDICHET, *Small Ball*, size 20, 4 boxes of *White, Beige or Ecru;*
or
ROYAL SOCIETY SIX CORD CORDICHET, *Large Ball*, size 20, 2 boxes of *White or Beige.*

MILWARD's steel crochet hook No. 8 or 9.

Each motif measures 4¼ inches.

First Motif... Ch 12, join to form ring. **1st rnd:** 24 sc in ring, join. **2nd rnd:** ch 4 (to count as tr); 2 more tr in same place as sl st, holding back the last loop of each st on hook; thread over and draw through all loops on hook, ch 1 tightly (cluster); * make 5 more ch, sk 2 sc; 3 tr in next sc, holding back the last loop of each st and completing as for previous cluster. Repeat from * around, ending with ch 5, join. **3rd rnd:** ch 12 (to count as sc and ch-11), * sc at tip of next cluster, ch 11. Repeat from *, joining last ch-11 to 1st ch of starting ch-12. **4th rnd:** * ch 5, sc in center ch of next loop, ch 5, sc in sc between loops. Repeat from * around, join. **5th rnd:** sl st to sc at tip of loop, ch 4, 4 more tr in same sc, * ch 9, 5 tr in sc at tip of next loop. Repeat from *, joining last ch-9 to 4th st of starting ch-4. **6th rnd:** ch 4; * tr in each of next 4 tr, holding back the last loop of each st; thread over and draw through all loops on hook; ch 1 tightly (a 5-tr cluster); make 8 more ch, sc in next loop, ch 8, tr in 1st tr of next tr-group, holding back the last loop. Repeat from *, joining last ch-8 to tip of 1st cluster. **7th rnd:** ch 6 (to count as dc and ch-3), dc in same place as sl st, * ch 8, sc in next loop, sc in sc, sc in following loop, ch 8; at tip of next cluster make dc, ch 3 and dc. Repeat from * around, joining last ch-8 to 3rd st of starting ch-6. **8th rnd:** sl st in ch-3, ch 6, in same ch-3 make dc; * ch 8, sc in next loop, sc in next 3 sc and in following loop, ch 8; in ch-3 sp make dc, ch 3 and dc. Repeat from * around. Join and break off.

Second Motif... Work as for first motif to 7th rnd incl. **8th rnd:** sl st in ch-3, ch 6, in same ch-3 make dc; ch 8, sc in next loop, sc in next 3 sc and in following loop, ch 8, dc in ch-3 sp, ch 1, sc in a ch-3 sp on first motif, ch 1, dc back in ch-3 sp on motif in work. Ch 8 and continue to next point, as for first motif, joining ch-3 to first motif as before —*always be sure motifs are joined so that they are right side up.* Complete rnd as for first motif, with no more joinings.

Make necessary number of motifs, always joining 2 points at each side to corresponding points of adjacent motifs.

For a tablecloth about 60 x 81 inches, 14 motifs across and 19 down.

Fill-in-lace... **1st rnd:** Same as 1st rnd of motif. **2nd rnd:** ch 4 and complete a 3-tr cluster, make 5 more ch, sc in any of the 8 free loops in space between joinings, * ch 5, sk 2 sc, 3-tr cluster in next sc, ch 5, sc in next free loop. Repeat from * around. Join and break off.

A background of splendor for your choicest table settings—this cloth of pointed wheels is gossamer and effective!

Northern Lights

MATERIALS:

ROYAL SOCIETY SIX CORD CORDICHET, *Small Ball, size 30, 4 boxes of White or Beige, or 6 boxes of Ecru or any color;* or

ROYAL SOCIETY SIX CORD CORDICHET, *Large Ball, size 30, 2 boxes of White or Beige.*

MILWARD'S steel crochet hook No. 11 or 12.

Each motif measures about 4½ inches in diameter, from point to point.

Motif . . . Starting at center, wind thread 5 times around forefinger (thus making a ring), and make 40 sc in ring. Join with sl st. **2nd rnd:** * ch 20, sc in next 5 sc. Repeat from * around; join (8 petals). **3rd rnd:** * 29 sc in loop, sk 2 sc, sc in next sc, sk 2 sc. Repeat from * around, join. **4th rnd:** sl st in each of next 9 sc of 1st petal, ** sc in next sc, * ch 5, sk 1 sc, sc in next sc. Repeat from * 4 more times, sk 9 sc of next petal and repeat from ** around; join. **5th rnd:** ch 12 (to count as d tr and ch-7), * sk 2 loops, sc in next (center) loop, ch 7, sk 2 loops, d tr between next 2 sc, ch 7. Repeat from * around; join. **6th rnd:** 9 sc in each sp; join. **7th rnd:** sl st in next 5 sc, ch 9, sc in 2nd ch from hook, 7 sc in ch-9, sc in last ch, ch 1, turn; sc in each sc across; turn; sl st in each st across. ** Ch 4, turn, * sk 1 st, dc in next st, ch 1. Repeat from * 2 more times, sk 1 st, dc in last st (4 ch-1 sps). Ch 1, turn; sc in each dc and sp across, sc in 3rd st of ch-4, ch 1, turn; sc in each st across, ch 1, turn; sc in each st across, ch 7, sc in 5th sc of next ch-7 sp, ch 1, turn; sc in last sc made, 7 sc in ch-7, sc in next sc, ch 1, turn; sc in each st across. Now repeat from ** around (16 sections completed). Fasten off.

Make necessary number of motifs and sew 2 points of each motif to 2 points of adjacent motifs, leaving 2 points free on each motif between joinings. For a tablecloth 54 x 72 inches, 12 motifs across and 16 down.

Fill-in-lace . . . Ch 10, join; * ch 16, sc in joining of 2 motifs, ch 16, sc in ring, (ch 11, sc in next free point of motif, ch 11, sc in ring) twice. Repeat from * around. Join and break off.

This motif is equally charming when used in making a doily, runner or vanity set.

Williamsburg

Tablecloth measures 60 x 80 inches. Motif measures 3¼ inches, point to point.

J. & P. COATS BEST SIX CORD MERCERIZED CROCHET, Art. A.104, Size 30: 42 balls of White; or
CLARK'S BIG BALL MERCERIZED CROCHET, Art. B.34, Size 30: 30 balls of White.
Milwards Steel Crochet Hook No. 10.

FIRST MOTIF . . . Starting at center, ch 10. Join with sl st to form ring. **1st rnd:** Ch 3, 23 dc in ring. Join with sl st to top of ch-3. **2nd rnd:** Ch 4, * dc in next dc, ch 1. Repeat from * around. Sl st in 3rd ch of ch-4. **3rd rnd:** Sc in next sp, * ch 7, skip next sp, sc in next sp. Repeat from * around, ending with ch 7, sl st in first sc. **4th rnd:** Sl st in next loop, ch 4, tr in same loop, * (ch 3, holding back on hook the last loop of each tr make 2 tr in same loop, thread over and draw through all loops on hook—cluster made) 3 times; ch 3, sc in next loop, ch 3, make a 2-tr cluster in next loop. Repeat from * around. Join last ch-3 to first tr made. **5th rnd:** Sl st in next sp, ch 4, tr in same sp, * ch 3, in next sp make a 2-tr cluster, ch 5 and 2-tr cluster; ch 3, cluster in next sp, ch 5, sc in next sc, ch 5, skip next sp, cluster in next sp. Repeat from * around. Join. **6th rnd:** Sl st in next ch, sc in same sp, * ch 5, in next sp make dc, ch 5 and dc; (ch 5, sc in next sp) 4 times. Repeat from * around. Join and break off.

SECOND MOTIF . . . Work as for First Motif until 5 rnds have been completed. **6th rnd:** Sl st in next ch, sc in same sp, ch 5, dc in next sp, ch 2, sl st in corresponding loop on First Motif, ch 2, dc in same sp on Second Motif, (ch 5, sc in next sp, ch 2, sl st in corresponding loop on First Motif, ch 2, sc in next sp on Second Motif) twice; ch 5, dc in next sp on Second Motif, ch 2, sl st in corresponding loop on First Motif, ch 2, dc in same sp on Second Motif. Complete rnd (no more joinings).

Make 13 rows of 32 motifs and 12 rows of 31 motifs, joining adjacent sides as Second Motif was joined to First Motif (where 3 corners meet, join 3rd corner to joining of previous 2 corners)—see diagram. Block to measurements.

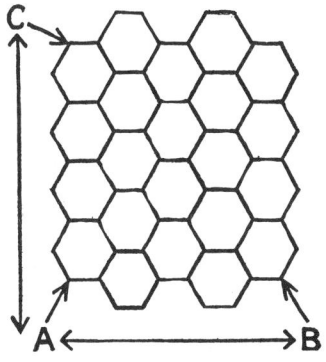

Diagram for Joining Hexagon Motifs

Enhance the intimate charm of your tea table with this lovely cloth in which daisy squares and blocks of fine linen alternate.

Lacy Daisy

MATERIALS:

ROYAL SOCIETY SIX CORD CORDICHET, *Small Ball, size 50, 2 boxes of White or Beige, or 3 boxes of Ecru; or*

ROYAL SOCIETY SIX CORD CORDICHET, *Large Ball, size 50, 1 box of White or Beige.*

MILWARD'S steel crochet hook No. 14.

1 yd. of linen, 36 inches wide.

Gauge: Each block measures 4¼ inches square.

Block ... Ch 8, join with sl st. **1st rnd:** ch 5, * dc in ring, ch 2. Repeat from * 6 more times, sl st in 1st ch-5 sp. **2nd rnd:** ch 3, 5 dc in same sp as sl st; * ch 1, 6 dc in next sp. Repeat from * 6 more times, ch 1, sl st in 3rd st of starting ch-3. **3rd rnd:** ch 3, dc in next 5 dc; * ch 2, dc in next 6 dc. Repeat from * 6 more times, ch 2, sl st in 3rd st of starting ch-3. **4th, 5th and 6th rnds:** same as 3rd rnd, making 1 more ch between dc-groups on each rnd. **7th rnd:** ch 3, dc in next 5 dc; * ch 11, dc in next 6 dc. Repeat from * 6 more times, ch 11, sl st in 3rd st of starting ch-3. **8th rnd:** * ch 3, ** dc in next 2 dc, holding back the last loop of each dc on hook; thread over and draw through all loops on hook. Repeat from ** once more, dc in next dc, ch 3, turn, sk 1 st, dc in next 2 sts, holding back the last loop of each dc; thread over and draw through all loops, ch 4, turn; sl st in 4th ch from hook (p); sl st along ch-3 and bar of dc, 8 sc in ch-11 loop, p, 8 sc in same loop, sl st in 1st dc. Repeat from * around. **9th rnd:** sl st to tip of 1st p, ch 19, d tr in same place as last sl st; * ch 9, h dc in next p, ch 7, sc in next p, ch 7, h dc in next p, ch 9, into next p make d tr, ch 13 and d tr. Repeat from * around, ending with ch 9, sl st in 6th ch of starting ch-19. **10th rnd:** * 17 sc in next loop (corner), sc in d tr, 11 sc in next loop, sc in h dc, 9 sc in next loop, sc in next sc, 9 sc in next loop, sc in h dc, 11 sc in next loop, sc in d tr. Repeat from * around. **11th rnd:** ch 9, * sk 8 sc, in next sc make tr, ch 11 and tr (corner); ch 5, sk 8 sc, tr in next st; ch 5, sk 5 sc, tr in next sc; ch 5, sk 5 sc, tr in next sc; ** ch 4, sk 4 sc, tr in next sc. Repeat from ** 3 more times, ch 5, sk 5 sc, tr in next sc, ch 5, sk 5 sc, tr in next sc, ch 5. Repeat from * around, ending with sl st in 4th ch of starting ch-9. **12th rnd:** ch 9, * tr in next tr, ch 5, sk 5 ch of corner, in next ch make tr, ch 11 and tr; (ch 5, tr in next tr) 4 times; ** ch 4, tr in next tr. Repeat from ** 3 more times, (ch 5, tr in next tr) twice; ch 5. Repeat from * around, sl st in 4th st of starting ch-9. **13th rnd:** ch 3, 5 dc in next sp, dc in next tr, 5 dc in next sp, dc in tr, * 5 dc in corner, 3 dc in 6th ch of same corner, 5 dc in same corner, dc in next tr, (5 dc in next sp, dc in next tr) 4 times; (4 dc in next sp, dc in next tr) 4 times; (5 dc in next sp, dc in next st) 4 times. Repeat from * around, sl st in 3rd st of ch-3. Fasten off. Make 60 more blocks.

Cut sixty 4½-inch squares of linen, and make a narrow hem all around (squares should now measure 4¼ inches). Alternate lace and linen squares to form a large square 11 x 11 blocks, having a lace block in each corner. Sew lace to linen.

Edging ... Starting at short side, ch 50 to measure 3¼ inches. **1st row:** tr in 14th ch from hook, * ch 4, sk 3 ch, tr in next ch. Repeat from * across (10 sps). Ch 9, turn. **2nd row:** * tr in next tr, ch 4. Repeat from * across. Ch 9, turn. Repeat 2nd row until piece measures the length of one side of cloth (47 inches). Work 10 more rows. Fasten off. Attach thread to tr preceding 10th sp at top of lace, ch 9 and work sps across the 10 extra rows (10 sps), thus starting lace for second side of cloth and, at the same time, forming a corner. Continue in this manner until lace is made for all sides of cloth. Fasten off. Sew the foundation chain to the top of the last 10 extra rows. Fasten off. **1st rnd:** Attach thread to 4th tr to right of one corner and make 4 sc in each sp around and 11 sc at corners. Join with sl st. **2nd rnd:** ch 4, tr in next 4 sc, (ch 10, sk 10 sc, tr in next 5 sc) twice, * ch 7, sk 7 sc, tr in next 5 sc. Repeat from * around, making corners as before, ending with ch-7, sl st in 4th st of starting ch-4. **3rd rnd:** ch 4, tr in next tr, * tr in next 2 tr, holding back the last loop of each tr on hook; thread over and draw through all loops on hook; tr in next tr, ch 10, tr in next 2 tr. Repeat from * around, ending with ch-10, sl st in 4th st of starting ch-4. **4th rnd:** * ch 4, tr in each of next 3 sts, holding back the last loop of each tr on hook; thread over and draw through all loops on hook (cluster); ch 5, sl st in tip of cluster (p), ch 4, sl st at base of last tr; into ch-10 loop make 5 sc, ch-5 p, and 5 sc. Repeat from * around. Fasten off. Sew edging to cloth with neat over and over sts.

Lattice Link

56 Inches Square

MATERIALS: J. & P. Coats Big Ball Best Six Cord Mercerized Crochet, *Size 20: 18 balls of White, Ecru or Cream,* or Clark's Big Ball Three Cord Mercerized Crochet, *Size 20: 15 balls of White, Ecru or Cream* . . . Steel Crochet Hook No. 9.

GAUGE: Each motif measures 1⅞ inches square.

FIRST MOTIF . . . 1st rnd: Ch 5, holding back on hook the last loop of each tr make 2 tr in 5th ch from hook, thread over and draw through all loops on hook (cluster made); (ch 5, cluster in 5th ch from hook) 3 times; sl st at base of first cluster. **2nd rnd:** Ch 4, cluster in same place as sl st, * ch 5, sc in center of side of next cluster on last rnd, ch 5, make a 3-tr cluster between next 2 clusters on last rnd. Repeat from * around. Sl st in tip of first cluster. **3rd rnd:** Ch 4, 2-tr cluster in same place as sl st, * ch 4, sl st in tip of cluster (picot made); ch 8, sl st in 5th st of ch-8, ch 4, make a 3-tr cluster in same place as last cluster was made, ch 4, sl st in tip of last cluster (another picot made), ch 4, d tr in next sc, ch 4, 3-tr cluster in tip of next cluster. Repeat from * around. Break off.

SECOND MOTIF . . . Work as for First Motif until 2nd rnd is completed. **3rd rnd:** Ch 4, 2-tr cluster in same place as sl st, picot, ch 6, sl st in corner picot on First Motif, ch 2, sl st in 2nd ch from joining on Second Motif, ch 4, 3-tr cluster in same place as last cluster was made on Second Motif, ch 2, sl st in corresponding picot on First Motif, ch 2, sl st in tip of last cluster on Second Motif, ch 4, d tr in next sc, ch 4, 3-tr cluster in tip of next cluster, ch 2, sl st in corresponding picot on First Motif, ch 2, sl st in tip of last cluster on Second Motif, ch 6, sl st in corner picot on First Motif, ch 2, sl st in 2nd ch from joining on Second Motif, ch 4, cluster in same place as last cluster on Second Motif and complete rnd as for First Motif (no more joinings).

Make 30 rows of 30 motifs, joining adjacent sides as Second Motif was joined to First Motif.

Bumblebee

45 x 60 Inches

MATERIALS: J. & P. Coats Big Ball Best Six Cord Mercerized Crochet, Size 30: 30 balls of White, Ecru or Cream, or 37 balls of any color, or Clark's Big Ball Three Cord Mercerized Crochet, Size 30: 22 balls of White, Ecru or Cream, or 30 balls of any color ... Steel Crochet Hook No. 10.

GAUGE: Each motif measures 2½ inches square.

FIRST MOTIF ... Starting at center, ch 12. Join with sl st to form ring. **1st rnd:** Ch 3, 4 dc in ring, (ch 9, 5 dc in ring) 3 times; ch 9, sl st in top of ch-3. **2nd rnd:** Ch 3, dc in next 2 dc, * ch 2, dc in same place as last dc. dc in next 2 dc, ch 2, in corner loop make 3 dc, ch 5 and 3 dc; ch 2, dc in next 3 dc. Repeat from * around. Join. **3rd rnd:** Ch 3, dc in next 2 dc, * ch 3, dc in next 6 dc, ch 3, in corner loop make 3 dc, ch 5 and 3 dc; ch 3, dc in next 6 dc. Repeat from * around. Join. **4th rnd:** Ch 3, dc in next 5 dc, * ch 5, skip 3 dc, dc in next 3 dc, ch 3, in corner loop make 3 dc, ch 5 and 3 dc; ch 3, dc in next 3 dc, ch 5, skip 3 dc, dc in next 6 dc. Repeat from * around. Join. **5th rnd:** Ch 3, holding back on hook the last loop of each dc make dc in next 5 dc, thread over and draw through all loops on hook (cluster made), * ch 12, skip 3 dc, dc in next 3 dc, ch 3, in corner loop make 3 dc, ch 7 and 3 dc; ch 3, dc in next 3 dc, ch 12, skip next 3 dc, make a 6-dc cluster over next 6 dc. Repeat from * around. Join and break off.

SECOND MOTIF ... Work as for First Motif until 4th rnd is completed. **5th rnd:** Ch 3, make a 5-dc cluster over next 5 dc, ch 12, skip 3 dc, dc in next 3 dc, ch 3, 3 dc in corner loop, ch 3, sl st in corner loop of First Motif, ch 3, 3 dc in same corner loop on Second Motif, ch 1, sl st in corresponding sp on First Motif, ch 1, dc in next 3 dc on Second Motif, ch 6, sl st in corresponding sp on First Motif, ch 6, skip next 3 dc on Second Motif, make a cluster over next 6 dc on Second Motif, ch 6, sl st in corresponding sp on First Motif, ch 6, skip 3 dc on Second Motif, dc in next 3 dc, ch 1, sl st in corresponding sp on First Motif, ch 1, 3 dc in corner loop on Second Motif, ch 3, sl st in corresponding sp on First Motif, ch 3, 3 dc in same corner on Second Motif as last 3 dc were made and complete rnd as for First Motif (no more joinings).

Make 18 rows of 24 motifs, joining adjacent sides as Second Motif was joined to First Motif (where 4 corners meet, join 3rd and 4th corners to joining of previous 2 corners.

EDGING ... Attach thread where motifs are joined, * (ch 1, sc in next sp, ch 1, sc in next 2 dc, ch 4, sl st in last sc—picot made—sc in next dc) twice; in next sp make (ch 2, 2 sc, picot and sc) twice; ch 2, sc in tip of next cluster, picot, in next sp make (ch 2, 2 sc, picot and sc) twice; ch 2, (sc in next 2 dc, picot, sc in next dc, ch 1, sc in next sp, ch 1) twice; sc between motifs, picot. Repeat from * around. Join and break off.

Cavalier

60 x 80 Inches

MATERIALS: J. & P. Coats Big Ball Best Six Cord Mercerized Crochet, *Size 30: 45 balls of White, Ecru or Cream, or 55 balls of any color,* or Clark's Big Ball Three Cord Mercerized Crochet, *Size 30: 29 balls of White, Ecru or Cream, or 44 balls of any color* . . . *Steel Crochet Hook No. 10.*

GAUGE: Each motif measures 3¼ inches across.

FIRST MOTIF . . . Starting at center, ch 10. Join with sl st to form ring. **1st rnd:** Ch 3, 23 dc in ring. Sl st in top of ch-3. **2nd rnd:** Ch 3, dc in same place as sl st, * ch 2, skip next dc, 2 dc in next dc. Repeat from * around, ending with ch 2. Join. **3rd rnd:** Ch 3, dc in next dc, * ch 3, dc in next 2 dc. Repeat from * around. Join. **4th rnd:** Ch 3, dc in next dc, * ch 6, dc in next 2 dc. Repeat from * around. Join. **5th rnd:** Ch 3, dc in next dc, * ch 2, sc in next sp, ch 2, dc in next 2 dc, ch 5, 5 dc in next sp, ch 5, dc in next 2 dc. Repeat from * around. Join. **6th rnd:** Ch 3, dc in next dc, * ch 2, dc in next 2 dc, ch 5, 3 dc in next sp, dc in next 5 dc, 3 dc in next sp, ch 5, dc in next 2 dc. Repeat from * around. Join. **7th rnd:** Ch 3, holding back on hook the last loop of each dc make dc in next 3 dc, thread over and draw through all loops on hook (cluster made): * ch 4, 3 dc in next sp, dc in next 11 dc, 3 dc in next sp, ch 4, make a 4-dc cluster over next 4 dc. Repeat from * around. Sl st in tip of first cluster. Break off.

SECOND MOTIF . . . Work as for First Motif until 6th rnd is completed. **7th rnd:** Ch 3, and complete cluster as before, * ch 4, dc in next sp, sl st in corresponding dc on First Motif, 2 dc in same sp on Second Motif, dc in next 6 dc, sl st in corresponding dc on First Motif, dc in next 5 dc, 3 dc in next sp, sl st in corresponding dc on First Motif, ch 4, make a dc-cluster over next 4 dc and complete rnd as for First Motif.

Make 15 rows of 21 motifs and 14 rows of 20 motifs, joining adjacent sides as Second Motif was joined to First Motif. See page 15.

EDGING . . . Attach thread to first dc following joining of motif on one long side, ch 4, sc in same place as thread was attached, * (sc in next 8 dc, ch 4, sl st in last sc—picot made) twice; 4 sc in next sp, sc in next cluster, 4 sc in next sp, sc in next dc, picot. Repeat from * across one long side and work in this manner over corresponding parts all around outer edges of cloth. Join and break off.

Cathedral Windows

Materials Required — AMERICAN THREAD COMPANY "STAR" SIX CORD QUALITY MERCERIZED CROCHET COTTON, ARTICLE 77

51—250 Yd. Balls, White, Ivory, Cream or Medium Ecru.
Steel Crochet Hook No. 10.

Each Motif measures about 4½ inches. 252 Motifs 18 x 14 are required for cloth measuring about 63 x 81 inches.

Ch 8, join, ch 3 and work 19 d c into ring, join each row.

2nd Row. Ch 7, skip 1 d c, d c in next d c, * ch 4, skip 1 d c, d c in next d c, repeat from * 7 times, ch 4, sl st in 3rd st of ch to join.

3rd Row. Ch 1, * 2 s c in next mesh, ch 3, 2 s c in same mesh, repeat from * all around.

4th Row. * 7 d c in ch 3 of previous row, s c over d c of 2nd row, repeat from * all around.

5th Row: Slip st to center of shell, * ch 7, sl st in center of next shell, repeat from * all around.

6th Row. Ch 5, d c in 2nd st of 7 ch loop, * ch 2, skip 1 st, d c in next st, repeat from * all around. (40 meshes.)

7th Row. Ch 5, 2 tr c cluster st in first mesh, (cluster st * thread over twice, insert in st and work off 2 loops twice, repeat from *, thread over and work off all loops at one time) ch 5, skip 1 mesh, * s c in next mesh, ch 5, 2 tr c cluster in same mesh, ch 5, skip 1 mesh, repeat from * all around. (20 cluster sts.)

8th Row. Sl st to top of cluster, * ch 7, sl st in top of next cluster, repeat from * all around.

9th Row. Ch 4, skip 1 st of ch, d c in next st, * ch 1, skip 1 st, d c in next st, repeat from * all around, ch 1, join in 3rd st of ch. (80 meshes.)

10th Row. Ch 3, 1 d c in each of the next 10 meshes and 10 d c, ** ch 5, skip 2 meshes, s c in next d c, * ch 4, skip 2 meshes, s c in next d c, repeat from * twice, ch 5, skip 2 meshes, 1 d c in each of the next 11 d c and 10 meshes, repeat from ** twice, ch 5, skip 2 meshes, s c in next d c, * ch 4, skip 2 meshes, s c in next d c, repeat from * twice, ch 5, join.

11th Row. 1 s c in each d c and 2 s c over each 5 ch loop, ch 6, 5 d c popcorn st in next mesh, (popcorn st: 5 d c in mesh, drop loop from hook, insert in 1st d c made and pull loop through) ch 3, work a popcorn st in next 2 meshes with ch 3 between, ch 6, 2 s c over next ch, 1 s c in each d c, 2 s c over next ch, repeat all around ending row with 2 s c over 5 ch loop.

12th Row: 1 s c in each s c, 2 s c over 6 ch loop, ch 7, 5 d c popcorn st in next 2 loops with ch 3 between, ch 7, 2 s c over 6 ch loop, repeat all around.

Continued on page 27.

Magic Star

65 x 100 Inches

MATERIALS: J. & P. Coats Big Ball Best Six Cord Mercerized Crochet, Size 10: 54 balls of White or Ecru, or Clark's Big Ball Three Cord Mercerized Crochet, Size 10: 45 balls of White or Ecru . . . Steel Crochet Hook No. 8.

GAUGE: Each motif measures 5 inches across center (from scallop to scallop).

FIRST MOTIF . . . Starting at center, ch 12. Join with sl st to form ring. **1st rnd:** Ch 4, 35 tr in ring. Sl st in top of ch-4. **2nd rnd:** Ch 5, holding back on hook the last loop of each d tr make d tr in next 4 tr, thread over and draw through all loops on hook (cluster made), * ch 5, tr in next tr, ch 5, make a 5-d tr cluster in next 5 tr. Repeat from * around. Sl st in tip of first cluster. **3rd rnd:** Sc in same place as sl st, * ch 7, in next tr make (2-d tr cluster, ch 3) twice and 2-d tr cluster; ch 7, sc in tip of next cluster. Repeat from * around, ending with ch 7. Sl st in first sc. **4th rnd:** * 4 sc in next ch-7 loop, (ch 5, 2-tr cluster in tip of next cluster) 3 times; ch 5, 4 sc in next ch-7 loop. Repeat from * around. Sl st in first sc. **5th rnd:** Sl st in next 3 sc, ch 4, tr in same place as last sl st, * ch 9, 2-tr cluster in tip of next cluster, (ch 7, 2-tr cluster in tip of next cluster) twice; ch 9, holding back on hook the last loop of next 4 tr, make 2 tr in next sc, skip 6 sc, make 2 tr in next sc, thread over and draw through all loops on hook (joint cluster made). Repeat from * around. Sl st in first tr. Break off.

SECOND MOTIF . . . Work as for First Motif until 4th rnd is completed. **5th rnd:** Sl st in next 3 sc, ch 4, tr in same place as last sl st, ch 9, 2-tr cluster in tip of next cluster, ch 7, 2-tr cluster in tip of next cluster, ch 3, sl st in corresponding sp on First Motif, ch 3, 2-tr cluster in tip of next cluster on Second Motif, ch 4, sl st in corresponding sp on First Motif, ch 4, make a joint cluster as before on Second Motif, ch 4, sl st in corresponding sp on First Motif, ch 4, 2-tr cluster in tip of next cluster on Second Motif, ch 3, sl st in corresponding sp on First Motif, ch 3, 2-tr cluster in tip of next cluster on Second Motif, and complete rnd as for First Motif (no more joinings).

Make 9 rows of 20 motifs and 8 rows of 19 motifs, joining adjacent sides of motifs as Second Motif was joined to First Motif. See page 15.

EDGING . . . Attach thread in tip of first free cluster following any joining, sc in same place, * ch 4, sl st in last sc (picot made), ch 5, 2 sc in next sp, ch 5, sc in next cluster. Repeat from * around outer edge of each motif, making ch-5 over joinings between motifs. Join and break off.

Cathedral Windows

Continued from page 24.

13th Row. 1 s c in each s c, 2 s c over 7 ch loop, ch 8, popcorn st in next loop, ch 8, 2 s c over 7 ch loop, repeat all around.

14th Row. 1 s c in each s c, 2 s c over 8 ch loop, ch 7, d c in top of popcorn st, ch 2, d c in same space, ch 7, 2 s c over ch, repeat all around. Sew or crochet Motifs together at the single crochet sts.

Joining Motif. Ch 4, join to form a ring, ch 1, 8 s c in ring, join.

2nd Row. Ch 4, join to corner of 1 large Motif, ch 4, skip 1 st of ring, s c in next st, ch 4, join to corner of 2nd Motif, ch 4, skip 1 st of ring, s c in next st, continue until all Motifs are joined.

Edge. Join thread in 3rd st from corner of Motif, ch 5, skip 1 st, d c in next st, * ch 2, skip 1 st, d c in next st, repeat across Motif to corner, 2 d c with ch 2 between in corner of Motif, 2 d c with ch 2 between in corner of next Motif, repeat from * all around.

2nd Row. Ch 5, 2 tr c cluster in same mesh, * ch 5, skip 1 mesh, sl st in next mesh, ch 5, 2 tr c cluster in same mesh, repeat from * all around.

Pagoda

60 x 80 Inches

MATERIALS: J. & P. Coats Big Ball Best Six Cord Mercerized Crochet, *Size 30: 40 balls of White, Ecru or Cream, or 48 balls of any color,* or Clark's Big Ball Three Cord Mercerized Crochet, *Size 30: 29 balls of White, Ecru or Cream, or 39 balls of any color* . . . *Steel Crochet Hook No. 10.*

GAUGE: Each motif measures 3¼ inches across center.

FIRST MOTIF . . . Starting at center, ch 8. Join with sl st to form ring. **1st rnd:** Ch 4, 2 tr in ring, (ch 5, dc in top of last tr, 3 tr in ring) 5 times; ch 5, dc in top of last tr. Sl st in top of ch-4. **2nd rnd:** Ch 4, tr in next 2 tr, * ch 5, dc in top of last tr, sc in next loop (of last rnd), ch 5, dc in last sc, tr in next 3 tr. Repeat from * around. Sl st in top of ch-4. **3rd rnd:** Ch 4, holding back on hook the last loop of each tr make tr in next 2 tr, thread over and draw through all loops on hook (cluster made); * (ch 4, sc in next loop) twice; ch 4, make a 3-tr cluster over next 3 tr. Repeat from * around. Sl st in tip of first cluster. **4th rnd:** Sl st in sp, ch 4, 4 tr in same sp, * (5 tr in next sp) twice; ch 9, 5 tr in next sp. Repeat from * around. Sl st in top of ch-4. **5th rnd:** Sl st in next 2 tr, ch 4, tr in next 10 tr, * ch 9, sc in next loop, ch 9, skip 2 tr, tr in next 11 tr. Repeat from * around. Join. **6th rnd:** Sl st in next 2 tr, ch 4, tr in next 6 tr, * (ch 9, sc in next loop) twice; ch 9, skip 2 tr, tr in next 7 tr. Repeat from * around. Join and break off.

SECOND MOTIF . . . Work as for First Motif until 5th rnd is completed. **6th rnd:** Ch 4, tr in next 6 tr, ch 9, sc in next loop, ch 5, sc in corresponding loop on First Motif, ch 5, sc in next loop on Second Motif, ch 4, sc in next loop on First Motif, ch 4, skip 2 tr on Second Motif, tr in next 7 tr, ch 4, sc in next loop on First Motif, ch 4, sc in next loop on Second Motif, ch 5, sc in corresponding loop on First Motif, ch 5, sc in next loop on Second Motif and complete rnd as for First Motif (no more joinings).

Make 11 rows of 23 motifs and 10 rows of 24 motifs, joining adjacent sides as Second Motif was joined to First Motif (where 3 corners meet, join 3rd corner to joining of previous 2 corners). See page 15.

EDGING . . . Attach thread at joining of first two motifs and, working along one long side, * ch 9, sc in next free loop, ch 9, skip 2 tr, tr-cluster over next 3 tr, ch 4, sl st in tip of cluster (picot made); (ch 9, sc in next loop) 3 times; make a 3-tr cluster as before, picot, ch 9, sc in next loop, ch 9, sc at joining of motifs. Repeat from * across side and continue working in pattern as established over corresponding parts of each motif around. Join and break off.

This is the pet of women who wish to crochet a smart cloth in a hurry! It seems to go a mile a minute and the result is really lovely.

Mile-a-Minute

MATERIALS:

ROYAL SOCIETY SIX CORD CORDICHET, *Small Ball, size 20, 3 boxes of White or Beige, or 4 boxes of Ecru;* or

ROYAL SOCIETY SIX CORD CORDICHET, *Large Ball, size 20, 2 boxes of White or Beige.*

MILWARD'S steel crochet hook No. 5.

Gauge: 2 sps or 2 bls measure 1 inch.

Block . . . Starting at center, ch 10, join. **1st rnd:** ch 4 (to count as 1 tr), make 31 more tr in ring. Join to top of starting ch-4. **2nd rnd:** ch 7 (to count as last tr of corner bl, and following ch-3); * sk 3 tr, tr in next st (sp); make another sp, 8 more tr in same st as last tr (corner bl), ch 3. Repeat from * around, ending with 8 tr in joining sl st, join to 4th st of starting ch-7. **3rd rnd:** ch 7 and complete sp by making tr in next tr; 1 more sp, ch 3, tr in center tr of 9 corner tr (3 sps made); * 8 more tr for corner, ch 3, tr in last tr of 9 corner tr, make 3 more sps. Repeat from * around; join. **4th rnd:** ch 4, 3 tr in sp, tr in tr (bl); 2 bls over next 2 sps, ch 3, tr in corner st, ch 7, tr in same place as last tr, ch 3, tr in last tr of corner bl, 4 bls, and continue thus around. Complete motif, following chart. Each bl consists of 5 tr in all; each sp consists of tr, ch 3 and tr. Corner sps consist of tr, ch 7 and tr; corner bls consist of 9 tr.

For a tablecloth 60 x 80 inches, make 3 blocks across and 4 down; sew together neatly with over and over sts on wrong side. Work 2 rnds of tr all around cloth, increasing at corners to keep work flat.

This motif is equally charming when used in making a buffet set or luncheon set.

Blue Hills

Tablecloth measures 58 x 78 inches. Motif measures 2½ inches square.

J. & P. COATS BEST SIX CORD MERCERIZED CROCHET, Art. A.104, Size 30: 33 balls of Ecru; or

CLARK'S BIG BALL MERCERIZED CROCHET, Art. B.34, Size 30: 25 balls of No. 61 Ecru.

Milwards Steel Crochet Hook No. 10.

FIRST MOTIF . . . Starting at center, ch 12. Join with sl st to form ring. **1st rnd:** Ch 3, make 31 dc in ring. Join. **2nd rnd:** Ch 3, dc in next 3 dc, * ch 9, dc in next 4 dc. Repeat from * around, ending with ch 9, sl st in top of ch-3. **3rd rnd:** Ch 4, holding back on hook the last loop of each tr make tr in next 3 dc, thread over and draw through all loops on hook, * ch 10, sc in next loop, ch 10, holding back on hook the last loop of each tr make tr in next 4 dc, thread over and draw through all loops on hook (4-tr cluster made). Repeat from * around, ending with ch 10, sl st in tip of first cluster. **4th rnd:** Sl st in next 5 ch, sc in same loop, ch 12, sc in next loop, * (ch 12, 3-d tr cluster in next loop) twice (a corner loop made); (ch 12, sc in next loop) twice. Repeat from * around, ending with ch 12, sl st in first sc. Break off.

SECOND MOTIF . . . Work as for First Motif until 3 rnds have been completed. **4th rnd:** Sl st in next 5 ch, sc in same loop, ch 12, sc in next loop, ch 12, 3-d tr cluster in next loop, ch 6, sl st in 6th ch of any corner loop on First Motif, ch 6, 3-d tr cluster in next loop on Second Motif, (ch 6, sl st in 6th ch of corresponding loop on First Motif, ch 6, sc in next loop on Second Motif) twice; ch 6, sl st in 6th ch of corresponding loop on First Motif, ch 6, a 3-d tr cluster in next loop on Second Motif, ch 6, sl st in 6th ch of corresponding corner loop on First Motif, ch 6, 3-d tr cluster in next loop on Second Motif. Complete as for First Motif (no more joinings). Break off.

Make 23 rows of 31 motifs, joining adjacent sides as Second Motif was joined to First Motif (where 4 corners meet, join 3rd and 4th corners to joining of previous 2 corners).

EDGING . . . **1st rnd:** Attach thread to any corner loop, sc in same place, * ch 12, sc in same loop, ** (ch 12, sc in next loop) 3 times; ch 12, sc in next joining. Repeat from ** across side, ending with sc in corner loop. Repeat from * around, ending with sl st in first sc. **2nd rnd:** In each loop around make 5 sc, (ch 5 and 3 sc) twice; ch 5 and 5 sc. Join and break off. Block to measurements.

Flower Show

60 x 82 Inches

MATERIALS: J. & P. Coats Big Ball Best Six Cord Mercerized Crochet, Size 30: 40 balls of White, Ecru or Cream, or 48 balls of any color, or Clark's Big Ball Three Cord Mercerized Crochet, Size 30: 29 balls of White, Ecru or Cream, or 39 balls of any color ... Steel Crochet Hook No. 10.

GAUGE: Each motif measures 3½ inches in diameter.

FIRST MOTIF ... Starting at center, ch 8. Join with sl st to form ring. **1st rnd:** 16 sc in ring. Sl st in first sc. **2nd rnd:** Ch 4, (dc in next sc, ch 1) 15 times. Sl st in 3rd st of starting chain. **3rd rnd:** Ch 5, * dc in next dc, ch 2. Repeat from * around. Sl st in 3rd st of starting chain. **4th rnd:** Ch 3, * 2 dc in next sp, dc in next dc, ch 5, dc in next dc. Repeat from * around. Join. **5th rnd:** Ch 3, dc in same place as sl st, * dc in next 2 dc, 2 dc in next sp, ch 3, sc in next sp, ch 3, 2 dc in next dc. Repeat from * around. Join. **6th rnd:** Ch 4, holding back on hook the last loop of each tr make tr in next 5 dc, thread over and draw through all loops on hook (cluster made), * ch 11, make a 6-tr cluster over next 6 dc. Repeat from * around, ending with ch 11, sl st in first cluster. **7th rnd:** Ch 8, dc in same place as sl st, * ch 3, 5 dc in next sp, ch 3, in tip of next cluster make dc, ch 5 and dc. Repeat from * around. Join with sl st to 3rd ch of ch-8. **8th rnd:** Ch 6, * sc in next sp, ch 3, dc in next dc, ch 3, 2 dc in next dc, dc in next 3 dc, 2 dc in next dc, ch 3, dc in next dc, ch 3. Repeat from * around. Sl st in 3rd st of ch-6. **9th rnd:** Sl st in next ch, sc in same sp, * ch 4, sc in next sp, ch 10, skip next dc, make a 7-tr cluster over next 7 dc, ch 10, skip next sp, sc in next sp. Repeat from * around. Sl st in next sc. Break off.

SECOND MOTIF ... Work as for First Motif until 8th rnd is completed. **9th rnd:** Sl st in next ch, sc in same sp, ch 4, sc in next sp, ch 10, tr-cluster over next 7 dc, ch 5, sl st in corresponding loop on First Motif, ch 5, skip 1 sp on Second Motif, sc in next sp, ch 4, sc in next sp, ch 5, sl st in corresponding sp on First Motif, ch 5, make a tr-cluster over next 7 dc, ch 10, skip 1 sp, sc in next sp, and complete rnd as for First Motif (no more joinings).

Make 17 rows of 23 motifs, joining motifs as Second Motif was joined to First Motif, having two ch-10 loops free between joinings.

FILL-IN MOTIF ... 1st rnd: Attach thread to first free ch-10 sp on a motif following joining, ch 4, 2 tr in same sp, * ch 5, d tr in ch-4 sp, ch 5, 3 tr in next ch-10 sp, ch 2, 3 tr in next free ch-10 sp on next motif. Repeat from * around. Sl st in top of ch-4. **2nd rnd:** Ch 4, make a 2-tr cluster over next 2 tr, * ch 8, (make a 3-tr cluster over next 3 tr) twice. Repeat from * around, ending with cluster over last 3 tr, sl st in first cluster. **3rd rnd:** Ch 5, holding back on hook the last loop of each d tr (make d tr between next 2-cluster groups) 3 times. Join and break off. Work Fill-in Motifs in this manner in all sps between joinings.

EDGING ... Attach thread at joining of any 2 motifs, sc in same place, * ch 4, (sc in next cluster, ch 4, sl st in last sc—picot made—ch 6, sc in next sp, ch 6, sc in next sp, picot, ch 6, sc in next sp, ch 6) 3 times; sc in next cluster, picot, ch 4, sc in joining of motifs. Repeat from * around. Join and break off.

Daisy Chain

60 x 80 Inches

MATERIALS: J. & P. Coats Big Ball Best Six Cord Mercerized Crochet, Size 30: 39 balls of White, Ecru or Cream, or 47 balls of any color, or Clark's Big Ball Three Cord Mercerized Crochet, Size 30: 22 balls of White, Ecru or Cream, or 38 balls of any color . . . Steel Crochet Hook No. 10.

GAUGE: Each motif measures 2½ inches across center.

FIRST MOTIF . . . Starting at center, ch 12. Join with sl st to form ring. **1st rnd:** Ch 5, 3 dc in ring, (ch 2, 3 dc in ring) 6 times; ch 2, 2 dc in ring. Sl st in 3rd ch of ch-5. **2nd rnd:** Sc in next sp, (ch 7, holding back on hook the last loop of each tr make tr in next 3 dc, thread over and draw through all loops on hook—cluster made—ch 7, sc in next ch-2 sp) 7 times; ch 7, cluster, ch 3, tr in first sc. **3rd rnd:** (Ch 5, sc in next loop) 15 times; ch 2, dc in tr. **4th rnd:** Ch 4, 2-tr cluster in same loop, * ch 5, sc in next loop, ch 5, in next loop make 3-tr cluster, ch 5 and 3-tr cluster. Repeat from * around, ending with a 3-tr cluster in loop formed by ch-2 and dc; ch 5, sl st in tip of first cluster. **5th rnd:** Sl st in next 2 ch, sl st in same loop, ch 4, tr in next loop, * ch 5, in next loop make 3-tr cluster, ch 5 and cluster; ch 5, holding back on hook the last loop of each tr make tr in each of next 2 loops, thread over and draw through all loops on hook (joint tr made). Repeat from * around. Join and break off.

SECOND MOTIF . . . Work as for First Motif until 4th rnd is completed. **5th rnd:** Sl st in next 2 ch, sl st in same loop, ch 4, tr in next loop, ch 5, 3-tr cluster in next loop, ch 2, sl st in corresponding loop on First Motif, ch 2, cluster in same loop on Second Motif as last cluster was made, ch 2, sl st in corresponding loop on First Motif, ch 2, make a joint tr as before on next 2 loops of Second Motif, ch 2, sl st in corresponding loop on First Motif, ch 2, cluster in next loop on Second Motif, ch 2, sl st in corresponding loop on First Motif, ch 2, cluster in same loop on Second Motif as last cluster was made and complete rnd as for First Motif (no more joinings).

Make 24 rows of 32 motifs, joining adjacent sides as Second Motif was joined to First Motif, leaving 2 loops free between joinings.

FILL-IN MOTIF . . . Attach thread in first free loop preceding joining, ch 5, * d tr in first free loop on next motif, ch 5, d tr in next loop. Repeat from * around, ending with ch 5, sl st in top of first ch-5. Break off. Work Fill-in Motifs in this manner in all sps between motifs.

EDGING . . . Attach thread to joining of any two motifs. ** Ch 8, * (2 sc in next free loop) twice; ch 5, cluster in next loop, ch 4, sl st in top of cluster (picot made), ch 5, cluster in same loop, picot, ch 5. Repeat from * once more, (2 sc in next sp) twice; ch 8, sc at joining of motifs. Repeat from ** around. Join and break off.

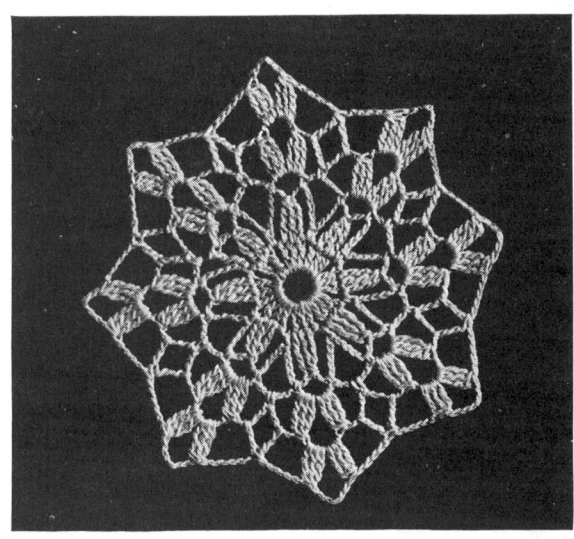

Orange Blossoms

MATERIALS:

Royal Society Six Cord Cordichet, *Small Ball*, size 30, 6 boxes of *White or Beige*, or 9 boxes of *Ecru or any color;* or

Royal Society Six Cord Cordichet, *Large Ball*, size 30, 3 boxes of *White or Beige*.

Milward's steel crochet hook No. 10 or 11.

Each motif measures 3¼ inches in diameter.

Motif . . . 1st rnd: ch 11, sl st in 6th ch from hook; * ch 2, 3 dc in ring, ch 2, sl st in ring. Repeat from * 4 more times (a flower made); ch 4, sk 4 ch of ch-11, dc in next ch. ** Ch 22, sl st in 6th ch from hook; working around, make ch 2, 3 dc in ring, ch 2, sl st in ring, ch 2, 2 dc in ring, sl st in center of 4th petal of last flower, dc in ring back on second flower, ch 2, sl st in ring. Make 3 more petals in same ring, ch 4, sk 4 ch of ch-22, dc in next ch. Repeat from ** 6 more times, joining 4th petal of last flower to second petal of first flower, thus forming a circle. Ch 11, remove hook, insert it in 1st ch at beginning of rnd and draw loop through. **2nd rnd:** ch 1, * in ch-12 loop make sc, h dc, 2 dc, h dc, 2 dc, 3 tr; to make a p, ch 4, sl st in 4th ch from hook; in same loop make 3 tr, 2 dc, h dc, 2 dc, h dc and sc. Sc in next st, in next sp make sc, p and sc; sc in next st. Repeat from * around. Fasten off. **3rd rnd:** ch 1 very loosely (this is center), ch 6 tightly. Sl st in 2nd dc of one free petal of a flower, * ch 6, sl st in center, ch 6, sl st in 2nd dc of next free petal. Repeat from * around, ending with sl st in center. Fasten off.

Make another motif to within first p of 2nd rnd. Then ch 1, sl st in corresponding p of first motif, ch 1, sl st in last tr of second motif, and continue as for 2nd rnd of first motif, joining next p of ch-12 loop to adjacent p of first motif. Complete rnd as for first motif.

Make necessary number of motifs, joining 2 points of each motif to 2 points of adjacent motifs.

For a tablecloth about 62 x 82 inches, 19 motifs across and 25 down.

Fill-in-lace . . . Ch 1 loosely (this is center), * ch 16 tightly; sl st in same place as joining, ch 16, sl st in center, ch 14, sl st in free p (between joinings), ch 14, sl st in center. Repeat from * around. Fasten off.

This motif is equally charming when used in making a chair set or runner.

Nantucket

Luncheon cloth measures 68 inches square. Motif measures 1⅞ inches square.

J. & P. COATS BEST SIX CORD MERCERIZED CROCHET, Art. A.104, Size 30: 24 balls of White; or

CLARK'S BIG BALL MERCERIZED CROCHET, Art. B.34, Size 30: 15 balls of White.

Milwards Steel Crochet Hook No. 10.

FIRST MOTIF . . . 1st rnd: Starting at center, ch 4, dc in 4th ch from hook, (ch 3, dc in last dc made) 7 times; sl st in first ch of ch-4. **2nd rnd:** Ch 3, 4 dc in same place as sl st, * ch 5, skip 1 dc, 5 dc in top of next dc. Repeat from * around. Join. **3rd rnd:** Ch 3, dc in next dc, * 5 dc in next dc, dc in next 2 dc, ch 5, skip 2 ch, d tr in next ch, ch 5, dc in next 2 dc. Repeat from * around. Join. **4th rnd:** Sl st in next 3 dc, ch 3, dc in same place as last sl st, * dc in next dc, ch 3, sl st in last dc made (picot made), dc in same place as last dc, 2 dc in next dc, ch 6, skip 4 ch, dc in next ch, in next d tr make 3 dc, a ch-4 picot and 2 dc; dc in next ch, ch 6, skip 3 dc, 2 dc in next dc. Repeat from * around. Join and break off.

SECOND MOTIF . . . Work as for First Motif until 3 rnds have been completed. **4th rnd:** Sl st in next 3 dc, ch 3, dc in same place as last sl st, in next dc make dc, a ch-3 picot and dc; 2 dc in next dc, ch 6, skip 4 ch, dc in next ch, in next d tr make 3 dc, ch 2, sl st in corresponding picot on First Motif, ch 2, sl st in last dc made on Second Motif, 2 dc in same d tr, dc in next ch, ch 6 and complete rnd as for First Motif, joining next 2 picots to corresponding picots on First Motif.

Make 36 rows of 36 motifs, joining adjacent sides as Second Motif was joined to First Motif, (where 4 corners meet, join 3rd and 4th corners to joining of previous 2 corners). Block to measurements.

Vintage

MATERIALS:

Royal Society Six Cord Cordichet, *Small Ball*, size 30, 8 boxes of *White or Beige*, or 12 boxes of *Ecru or any color;* or
Royal Society Six Cord Cordichet, *Large Ball*, size 30, 4 boxes of *White or Beige*.

Milward's steel crochet hook No. 10 or 11.

Gauge: 6 sps make 1 inch; 6 rows make 1 inch. Tablecloth measures about 74 x 90 inches.

Corner Scallop . . . Starting at A on chart, ch 75 (18 ch sts to 1 inch). **1st row:** dc in 4th ch from hook and in each ch (73 dc, counting turning ch as 1 dc). Ch 17, turn. **2nd row:** dc in 4th ch from hook and in each ch; dc in next dc, ch 2, sk 2 dc, dc in next

dc (1 sp); make 2 more sps, dc in next 12 dc (4 bls); 16 sps, dc in next 2 dc, dc in 3rd st of turning ch. Ch 3, turn. **3rd row:** 1 bl, 20 sps, dc in next 2 ch, dc in next dc, dc in next 2 ch, dc in next dc (2 bls); 5 sps, ch 2, foundation dc in turning ch (to make foundation dc, thread over, insert hook in ch and draw thread through; thread over and draw through one loop, making a ch st; complete as for dc). Make 8 more foundation dc and 1 dc in usual way, inserting hook in the ch st of previous foundation dc (3 bls increased). Ch 8, turn. **4th row:** dc in 4th ch from hook, dc in next 4 ch, dc in next dc; 7 sps, 2 bls, 22 sps, 1 bl. Ch 3, turn. **5th row:** 1 bl, 3 sps, 2 bls, 2 sps, 3 bls, 11 sps, 1 bl, 2 sps, 1 bl, 8 sps, increase 2 bls. Ch 5, turn. Starting at B, follow chart on page 6 until 15 rows are made; ch 2 and break off, leaving 6-inch thread.

Continued on page 46.

Motif Medley

ROYAL SOCIETY SIX CORD CORDICHET, Small Ball, Size 30: 70 balls of White or Ecru.
Steel Crochet Hook No. 10.

Each medallion measures about 2½ inches in diameter.

Completed cloth measures about 70 x 90 inches.

FIRST MOTIF . . . Starting at center, ch 8. Join with sl st to form ring. **1st rnd:** Ch 3; 19 dc in ring. Join with sl st in 3rd st of starting chain. **2nd rnd:** Ch 1, sc in same place as sl st, * ch 5, sc in next dc. Repeat from * around, joining last ch-5 with sl st in 1st sc. **3rd rnd:** Sl st to center of ch-5 loop, ch 1, sc in same loop, * ch 3, sc in next loop. Repeat from * around. Join. **4th rnd:** Sl st in ch-3 sp, ch 4, holding back on hook the last loop of each tr make 2 tr in same sp, thread over and draw through all loops on hook (a 2-tr cluster made), * ch 3, 3-tr cluster in next sp. Repeat from * around. Join with sl st in top of 1st cluster. **5th rnd:** Sl st in sp, ch 4, * in next sp make tr, ch 5, sl st in 3rd ch from hook, ch 2 and tr. Repeat from * around, ending with tr in same place as starting ch-4, ch 5, sl st in 3rd ch from hook, ch 2. Join with sl st in 4th st of starting chain. Break off.

SECOND MOTIF . . . Work same as First Motif until 4th rnd is complete. **5th rnd:** Sl st in sp, ch 4, (tr in next sp, ch 4, sl st in next p on First Motif, ch 1, sl st in 3rd st of last ch-4, ch 2, tr in same sp on Second Motif) twice; complete rnd with no more joinings. Break off.

THIRD MOTIF . . . Work same as First Motif until 4th rnd is complete. **5th rnd:** Sl st in sp, ch 4, tr in next sp, ch 4, skip 2 p's on Second Motif to the right of double joining, sl st in next p, ch 1, sl st in 3rd st of last ch-4, ch 2, tr in same sp on Third Motif, (in next sp make tr, ch 5, sl st in 3rd ch from hook,

Continued on page 46.

Festivity

Royal Society Cordichet, size 20, 7 boxes of White or 9 boxes of Ecru.
Milward's steel crochet hook No. 10.
Tablecloth, measuring 63 x 81 inches, is made of individual motifs, 4½ inches in diameter.

Starting at center, ch 5, join with sl st to form ring. **1st rnd:** ch 1, 11 sc in ring. Join rnd with sl st. **2nd rnd:** ch 10 (to count as dc and ch-7), * sk 2 sc, dc in next sc, ch 7. Repeat from * 2 more times, ch 5, h dc in 3rd st of starting ch-10. **3rd rnd:** ch 5, sk 1 ch of next ch-7 loop, * sc in each of next 5 ch, ch 5, sk next dc and 1 ch of next loop. Repeat from * around, ending with sc in each of last 5 ch, sl st in next ch-5 loop. **4th rnd:** ch 3 (to count as dc), 2 dc in same loop, ch 3, 3 dc in same loop, * ch 3, sk 2 sc, sc in next sc, ch 3; in next ch-5 make: 3 dc, ch 3, 3 dc. Repeat from * around. Join last ch-3 to 3rd st of starting ch. Hereafter pick up only back loop of each dc. **5th rnd:** ch 3, dc in each of next 2 dc, * dc in each of next 3 ch, dc in each of next 3 dc, ch 3, sc in next sp, ch 3, sc in next sp, ch 3, dc in each of next 3 dc. Repeat from * around. Join last ch-3 with sl st to 3rd st of starting ch. Turn. Hereafter work in rows over one loop-section as follows: **1st row:** ch 6 (to count as dc and ch-3), sc in first loop, ch 3, sc in next loop, sc in next loop, ch 3, dc in dc (4 loops in row); turn. **2nd row:** ch 6, sc in first loop, * ch 3, sc in next loop. Repeat from * 2 more times, ch 3, dc in 3rd st of turning ch (5 loops); turn. **3rd row:** sl st to center of 1st loop, * ch 3, sc in next loop. Repeat from * 3 more times (4 loops); turn. **4th row:** Same as 3rd row, but make 3 (instead of 4) loops; turn. **5th row:** Make 2 loops as in row below; turn. **6th row:** sl st to center of 1st loop, ch 2, h dc in next loop. Fasten and break off. Attach thread to last dc of dc-group, and work another loop-section same as this. Work remaining 2 loop-sections in same manner. Do not break off at end of last section, but work in rnds, taking care to have right side of work toward you. (Pick up only the back loop of each st throughout.)

1st rnd: sl st to center of top loop, ch 1, sc in same loop, * 2 sc in each of next 3 side loops, 5 sc in next loop, 2 sc in next loop, sc in each of next 7 dc, 2 sc in next side loop, 5 sc in next loop, 2 sc in each of next 3 side loops; in top loop make: 2 sc, ch 2, 2 sc. Repeat from * around, ending with ch 2, sl st in starting ch-1. **2nd rnd:** ch 1, sc in each of next 10 sc, * sk 5 sc, d tr in next sc (over 3rd dc of row below), ch 7, sk 1 sc; in next sc make a long tr tr (thread over hook 5 times); ch 7, sk 1 sc, d tr in next sc, sk 5 sc, sc in 3rd sc of next 5-sc group, sc in each sc to within top ch-2, sc in 1st ch, ch 2, sc in next ch, sc in each of next 11 sc. Repeat from * around, ending with

Continued on page 46.

Vintage

Continued from page 43.

Large Scallop . . . Ch 93 (18 ch sts to 1 inch). **1st row:** dc in 4th ch from hook and in each ch (91 dc). Ch 17, turn. **2nd row:** dc in 4th ch from hook and in each ch, dc in next dc, 3 sps, 4 bls, 7 sps, 2 bls, 7 sps, 4 bls, 2 sps, ch 2, foundation dc in turning ch; 14 more foundation dc and 1 dc in the usual way. Ch 11, turn. Starting at C, follow chart until 15 rows are made. Ch 2 and break off, leaving 6-inch thread. Using this thread, sew ch-2 of corner scallop to turning ch on last row of large scallop.

Small Scallop . . . Ch 48. **1st row:** dc in 4th ch from hook and in each ch. Ch 11, turn. Starting at D, follow chart until 6 rows are made. Ch 2 and break off. Sew ch-2 of large scallop to turning ch on last row of small scallop. Continue thus, alternating a large scallop and a small scallop until 4 large and 3 small scallops in all are joined. Make another corner scallop, starting at E on chart (to reverse this corner), and work until 15 rows are made. Do not break off but reverse corner and join to large scallop. Ch 3, turn. **16th row:** 1 bl, 4 sps, 2 bls, 3 sps, 2 bls, 1 sp, 5 bls, 8 sps, 3 bls, 1 sp, 1 bl, 1 sp, 2 bls, 1 sp, 1 bl, 5 sps, 2 bls. This brings work to F on chart; follow chart across. (The chart shows ¼ of design. To make second half of each row, repeat first half, starting at center and working back to beginning of row.) Ch 3, turn. Starting at 17th row, follow chart until 24 rows are made. **25th row:** sl st in 4 dc (1 bl decreased), ch 3 and follow chart across. Now follow chart to top row; then reverse chart and work back, completing scallops at bottom of chart individually.

Motif Medley

Continued from page 44.

ch 2 and tr) twice; tr in next sp, ch 4. skip 2 p's on First Motif to the right of double joining. sl st in next p, ch 1, sl st in 3rd st of last ch-4, ch 2, tr in same sp on Third Motif; complete rnd with no more joinings. Break off.

FOURTH MOTIF . . . Work same as First Motif until 4th rnd is complete. **5th rnd:** Sl st in sp, ch 4, tr in next sp, ch 4, skip 2 p's on Second Motif to the right of single joining, sl st in next p, ch 1, sl st in 3rd st of last ch-4, ch 2, tr in same sp on Fourth Motif, (in next sp make tr, ch 5, sl st in 3rd ch from hook, ch 2 and tr) twice; (tr in next sp, ch 4, skip 2 p's on Third Motif to the right of single joining, sl st in next p, ch 1, sl st in 3rd st of last ch-4, ch 2, tr in same sp on Fourth Motif) twice; complete rnd with no more joinings. Break off.

Make 1030 motifs in all and join them as in diagram. having 36 motifs on 1st row; 35 motifs on 2nd row; and 36 motifs on 3rd row. Repeat 2nd and 3rd rows until 29 rows in all are made.

FILL-IN-LACE . . . Attach thread to a p between motifs, ch 1, sc in same place where thread was attached, (ch 3, sc in next p) 5 times; ch 3, join with sl st in 1st sc. Break off. Fill in all sps between motifs in same way.

Festivity

Continued from page 45.

sc in top ch-1, ch 2, sc in next ch, sl st in starting ch-1. **3rd rnd:** ch 1 (to count as sc), sc in each st around, making ch-2 at tip of each of 8 points, and ending with sl st in starting ch-1. **4th rnd:** sl st back in ch-2 point, * ch 5, sk 5 sts, tr in next sc, ch 5, sk 5 sc, d tr in next sc, ch 5, sk 5 sc, tr in next sc, ch 5, sc in ch-2 at tip of next point. Repeat from * around, ending with sl st in 1st st of starting ch-5 (32 ch-5 sps). **5th rnd:** 6 sc in each ch-5 sp around. **6th and 7th rnds:** sc in each sc around. Join 7th rnd with sl st. **8th rnd:** ch 6 (to count as dc and ch-3), dc in same place as sl st, * ch 4, sk 3 sc, sc in next sc, ch 4, sk 3 sc; in next sc make: dc, ch 3, dc. Repeat from * around (24 scallops). Join and break off.

Place motifs in position, 14 motifs across and 18 down, 252 motifs. With over and over sts, sew 3 points of one motif to corresponding 3 points of adjacent motif (thus leaving 3 points free between joinings on each motif).

To make fill-in-lace between motifs, ch 5, join with sl st to form ring. * Ch 18, sc at joining of 2 motifs, ch 18, sc in center ring, ch 10, sc in point of next scallop, ch 10, sc in center ring, ch 8, sc in point of next scallop, ch 8, sc in center ring, ch 10, sc in point of next scallop, ch 10, sc in center ring. Repeat from * 3 more times. Join and break off. Make fill-in-lace in all sps between joinings of motifs.

SIMPLE CROCHET STITCHES

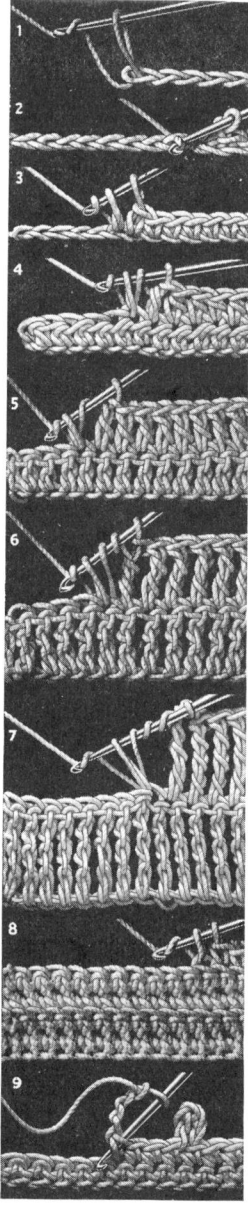

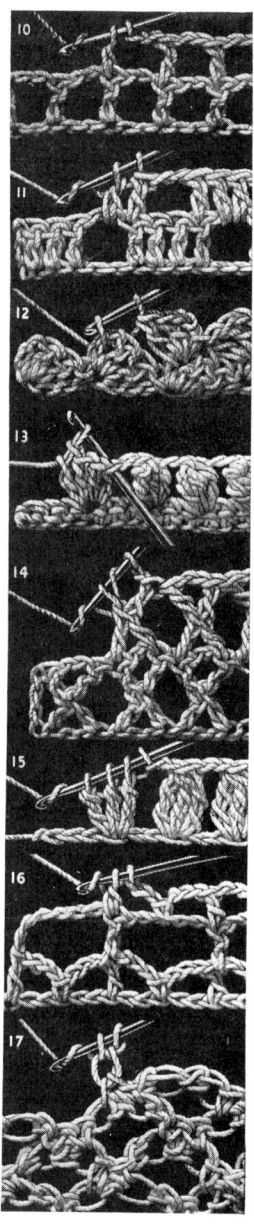

No. 1—Chain Stitch (CH) Form a loop on thread insert hook on loop and pull thread through tightening threads. Thread over hook and pull through last chain made. Continue chains for length desired.

No. 2—Slip Stitch (SL ST) Make a chain the desired length. Skip one chain, * insert hook in next chain, thread over hook and pull through stitch and loop on hook. Repeat from *. This stitch is used in joining and whenever an invisible stitch is required.

No. 3—Single Crochet (S C) Chain for desired length, skip 1 ch, * insert hook in next ch, thread over hook and pull through ch. There are now 2 loops on hook, thread over hook and pull through both loops, repeat from *. For succeeding rows of s c, ch 1, turn insert hook in top of next st taking up both threads and continue same as first row.

No. 4—Short Double Crochet (S D C) Ch for desired length thread over hook, insert hook in 3rd st from hook, draw thread through (3 loops on hook), thread over and draw through all three loops on hook. For succeeding rows, ch 2, turn.

No. 5—Double Crochet (D C) Ch for desired length, thread over hook, insert hook in 4th st from hook, draw thread through (3 loops on hook) thread over hook and pull through 2 loops thread over hook and pull through 2 loops. Succeeding rows, ch 3, turn and work next d c in 2nd d c of previous row. The ch 3 counts as 1 d c.

No. 6—Treble Crochet (TR C) Ch for desired length, thread over hook twice insert hook in 5th ch from hook draw thread through (4 loops on hook) thread over hook pull through 2 loops thread over, pull through 2 loops, thread over, pull through 2 loops. For succeeding rows ch 4, turn and work next tr c in 2nd tr c of previous row. The ch 4 counts as 1 tr c.

No. 7—Double Treble Crochet (D TR C) Ch for desired length thread over hook 3 times insert in 6th ch from hook (5 loops on hook) and work off 2 loops at a time same as tr c. For succeeding rows ch 5 turn and work next d tr c in 2nd d tr c of previous row. The ch 5 counts as 1 d tr c.

No. 8—Rib Stitch. Work this same as single crochet but insert hook in back loop of stitch only. This is sometimes called the slipper stitch.

No. 9—Picot (P) There are two methods of working the picot. (A) Work a single crochet in the foundation, ch 3 or 4 sts depending on the length of picot desired, sl st in top of s c made. (B) Work an s c, ch 3 or 4 for picot and s c in same space. Work as many single crochets between picots as desired.

No. 10—Open or Filet Mesh (O M.) When worked on a chain work the first d c in 8th ch from hook * ch 2, skip 2 sts, 1 d c in next st, repeat from *. Succeeding rows ch 5 to turn, d c in d c, ch 2, d c in next d c, repeat from *.

No. 11—Block or Solid Mesh (S M) Four double crochets form 1 solid mesh and 3 d c are required for each additional solid mesh. Open mesh and solid mesh are used in Filet Crochet.

No. 12—Slanting Shell St. Ch for desired length, work 2 d c in 4th st from hook, skip 3 sts, sl st in next st, * ch 3, 2 d c in same st with sl st, skip 3 sts, sl st in next st. Repeat from *. **2nd Row.** Ch 3, turn 2 d c in sl st, sl st in 3 ch loop of shell in previous row, * ch 3, 2 d c in same space, sl st in next shell, repeat from *.

No. 13—Bean or Pop Corn Stitch. Work 3 d c in same space, drop loop from hook insert hook in first d c made and draw loop through, ch 1 to tighten st.

No. 14—Cross Treble Crochet. Ch for desired length, thread over twice, insert in 5th st from hook, * work off two loops, thread over, skip 2 sts, insert in next st and work off all loops on needle 2 at a time, ch 2, d c in center to complete cross. Thread over twice, insert in next st and repeat from *.

No. 15—Cluster Stitch. Work 3 or 4 tr c in same st always retaining the last loop of each tr c on needle, thread over and pull through all loops on needle.

No. 16—Lacet St. Ch for desired length, work 1 s c in 10th st from hook, ch 3 skip 2 sts, 1 d c in next st, * ch 3, skip 2 sts, 1 s c in next st, ch 3, skip 2 sts 1 d c in next st, repeat from * to end of row, 2nd row, d c in d c, ch 5 d c in next d c.

No. 17—Knot Stitch (Sometimes Called Lovers Knot St.) Ch for desired length, * draw a ¼ inch loop on hook, thread over and pull through ch, s c in single loop of st, draw another ¼ inch loop, s c into loop, skip 4 sts, s c in next st, repeat from *. To turn make ⅜" knots, * s c in loop at right of s c and s c in loop at left of s c of previous row, 2 knot sts and repeat from *.

METRIC CONVERSION CHART

CONVERTING INCHES TO CENTIMETERS AND YARDS TO METERS

mm — millimeters cm — centimeters m — meters

INCHES INTO MILLIMETERS AND CENTIMETERS
(Slightly rounded off for convenience)

inches	mm		cm	inches	cm	inches	cm	inches	cm
1/8	3mm			5	12.5	21	53.5	38	96.5
1/4	6mm			5½	14	22	56	39	99
3/8	10mm	or	1cm	6	15	23	58.5	40	101.5
1/2	13mm	or	1.3cm	7	18	24	61	41	104
5/8	15mm	or	1.5cm	8	20.5	25	63.5	42	106.5
3/4	20mm	or	2cm	9	23	26	66	43	109
7/8	22mm	or	2.2cm	10	25.5	27	68.5	44	112
1	25mm	or	2.5cm	11	28	28	71	45	114.5
1¼	32mm	or	3.2cm	12	30.5	29	73.5	46	117
1½	38mm	or	3.8cm	13	33	30	76	47	119.5
1¾	45mm	or	4.5cm	14	35.5	31	79	48	122
2	50mm	or	5cm	15	38	32	81.5	49	124.5
2½	65mm	or	6.5cm	16	40.5	33	84	50	127
3	75mm	or	7.5cm	17	43	34	86.5		
3½	90mm	or	9cm	18	46	35	89		
4	100mm	or	10cm	19	48.5	36	91.5		
4½	115mm	or	11.5cm	20	51	37	94		

YARDS TO METERS
(Slightly rounded off for convenience)

yards	meters	yards	meters	yards	meters	yards	meters	yards	meters
1/8	0.15	2 1/8	1.95	4 1/8	3.80	6 1/8	5.60	8 1/8	7.45
1/4	0.25	2¼	2.10	4¼	3.90	6¼	5.75	8¼	7.55
3/8	0.35	2 3/8	2.20	4 3/8	4.00	6 3/8	5.85	8 3/8	7.70
1/2	0.50	2½	2.30	4½	4.15	6½	5.95	8½	7.80
5/8	0.60	2 5/8	2.40	4 5/8	4.25	6 5/8	6.10	8 5/8	7.90
3/4	0.70	2¾	2.55	4¾	4.35	6¾	6.20	8¾	8.00
7/8	0.80	2 7/8	2.65	4 7/8	4.50	6 7/8	6.30	8 7/8	8.15
1	0.95	3	2.75	5	4.60	7	6.40	9	8.25
1 1/8	1.05	3 1/8	2.90	5 1/8	4.70	7 1/8	6.55	9 1/8	8.35
1¼	1.15	3¼	3.00	5¼	4.80	7¼	6.65	9¼	8.50
1 3/8	1.30	3 3/8	3.10	5 3/8	4.95	7 3/8	6.75	9 3/8	8.60
1½	1.40	3½	3.20	5½	5.05	7½	6.90	9½	8.70
1 5/8	1.50	3 5/8	3.35	5 5/8	5.15	7 5/8	7.00	9 5/8	8.80
1¾	1.60	3¾	3.45	5¾	5.30	7¾	7.10	9¾	8.95
1 7/8	1.75	3 7/8	3.55	5 7/8	5.40	7 7/8	7.20	9 7/8	9.05
2	1.85	4	3.70	6	5.50	8	7.35	10	9.15

AVAILABLE FABRIC WIDTHS

25"	65cm	50"	127cm
27"	70cm	54"/56"	140cm
35"/36"	90cm	58"/60"	150cm
39"	100cm	68"/70"	175cm
44"/45"	115cm	72"	180cm
48"	122cm		

AVAILABLE ZIPPER LENGTHS

4"	10cm	10"	25cm	22"	55cm
5"	12cm	12"	30cm	24"	60cm
6"	15cm	14"	35cm	26"	65cm
7"	18cm	16"	40cm	28"	70cm
8"	20cm	18"	45cm	30"	75cm
9"	22cm	20"	50cm		